jB   c.1
 Au2a
Ayars
    John James Audubon: bird artist

The Discovery Books are prepared

under the educational supervision of

Mary C. Austin, Ed.D.

Reading Specialist and

Professor of Education

Western Reserve University

A DISCOVERY BOOK

GARRARD PUBLISHING COMPANY
CHAMPAIGN, ILLINOIS

John James Audubon:

Bird Artist

by James Sterling Ayars

illustrated by George I. Parrish

For two who gave help beyond

measure—Lucy and Becky

Contents

John James Audubon: Bird Artist

CHAPTER

1   The Parrot Mignonne . . .   7

2   The Book of Birds 11

3   The Museum 17

4   Off to Study 21

5   Off to Mill Grove 29

6   The Bakewells 37

7   Storekeeper Audubon . . . 45

8   Hard Times 53

9   In Search of a Printer . . 59

10 A Printer Found 63

11 Success at Last 73

c. 1

Chapter *1*

The Parrot Mignonne

Fougère was up early. He tiptoed through the hall and into one of the rooms of his new home.

Monkeys slept on the floor. Parrots sat quietly on their perches. The parrots were very beautiful. They were green and blue, yellow and red. One of them was named Mignonne. She reminded Fougère of the parrots in his old home in Santo Domingo, across the sea.

Santo Domingo is now called Haiti. Fougère was born there in 1785.

Fougère was four years old when he and his father and his little sister Rosa left Santo Domingo. They came to live in Nantes, a city on the west coast of France.

Fougère's father was Jean Audubon, a French sea captain and merchant. Captain Audubon's ships carried sugar, coffee and cotton from Santo Domingo to France. They carried cloth and other things from France to Santo Domingo.

Fougère's mother had died in Santo Domingo. In Nantes, Fougère had a new mother. She was kind to him, and he liked her very much.

As Fougère watched the parrots, he heard footsteps in the hall. A servant walked into the room bringing food for the parrots and monkeys.

The monkeys started squealing. The parrots started talking. They wanted their breakfasts.

Mignonne called, *"Du pain au lait pour le perroquet Mignonne!"* She was saying, "A roll for the parrot Mignonne!"

One of the big monkeys did not like Mignonne. Her talking made him angry. He glared at her. Suddenly, he grabbed her. Before the servant could stop him, the monkey killed the beautiful parrot.

Fougère stared at the dead bird. At first, he was so shocked that he could not say a word. When he could talk, he begged the servant to punish the monkey.

The servant liked the monkey. He would not punish him.

Fougère burst into tears. His mother heard him and rushed into the room.

She tried very hard to comfort him. She promised that Mignonne would be buried in the garden and that a pretty stone should be placed on her grave.

After a while, Fougère stopped crying.

Many years later, Fougère became known as John James Audubon, a very famous painter of birds. Though he painted pictures of many other birds, he never forgot the parrot Mignonne.

Chapter *2*

The Book of Birds

When Fougère came to Nantes with his father and sister, many French people were fighting against their king. They wanted to be free to rule themselves.

One day when Fougère was about eight years old, he heard shooting in the streets. Many people were hurt. Some were killed.

Captain Audubon was one of the people fighting against the French king. A few years before, he had fought with the American colonists against the British in the Revolutionary War.

After that war, Captain Audubon had lived for a few months in the United States. He admired the American people and their love of freedom.

The Captain wanted to get his wife and children away from the fighting in Nantes. So he moved them to a peaceful village nearby.

Fougère loved the village. Close to it were fields and woods where he could go to look at birds.

One day when Fougère and his father went for a walk in the fields, they found a bird's nest. Fougère stood and looked at the eggs for a long time.

"These eggs are like flowers still in bud," Captain Audubon told Fougère. "Someday they will become birds, just as buds become flowers."

Fougère's father showed him many things. He showed him where to find birds' nests. He told him how birds fly south in autumn and north in spring.

Fougère liked the birds so much that he wanted to take them home with him.

The Captain asked, "How could you take them home without killing them?"

Fougère did not know what to say. He wanted to have the birds close to him. But he did not want to kill them.

A short time later, Captain Audubon put a book into Fougère's hands. In the book were many pictures of birds.

Slowly Fougère turned the pages of the book. Suddenly he knew how he could take birds home without killing them. He could draw pictures of them. He could take them home on paper.

"*A new life ran in my veins,*" Fougère wrote many years later as he remembered that day.

After that, Fougère went often into the fields and woods to draw pictures of birds. He tried to make each drawing better than the one before.

Captain Audubon and his friends said that Fougère's drawings were very good. Fougère wanted them to be still better.

"These drawings," he said to his father, "make the birds look like a family of cripples."

Before he was fourteen, Fougère had made hundreds of drawings of birds. But he did not think his drawings were good enough to keep. On some of his birthdays, he made bonfires of them.

Chapter *3*

The Museum

Fougère looked about his room with pride. Birds' nests, birds' eggs, plants and rocks were neatly placed on shelves and tables.

"It makes quite a show," he thought.

While Captain Audubon had been at sea, Fougère had turned his room into a museum. Almost every day, instead of going to school, he had wandered in the fields and woods. Almost every day he had brought back something for the museum.

Now his father was coming home. Fougère would show him the museum.

Footsteps sounded in the hall, and seconds later the Captain walked into the room. He looked over the birds' nests, the eggs, the plants and the rocks.

"Very good! Very good!" he said. Then he asked, "And what have you done in school while I have been so long away?"

Fougère hung his head. He did not answer. Without saying another word, Captain Audubon left the room.

After dinner that evening, the Captain asked Rosa to play her violin. Rosa played so well that Captain Audubon gave her a beautiful big book he had brought home.

"Now, Fougère!" the Captain said.

Slowly Fougère took his violin out of its case. One of the strings was broken.

The Captain looked at his wife.

"He has not been practicing," Madame Audubon said softly.

The Captain asked Fougère questions about his school lessons. Fougère could answer only a few of the questions.

"He has not been studying much," Madame Audubon said. She was very kindhearted. She did not make Fougère do what he did not want to do.

Captain Audubon had a quick temper. At times it was like a hurricane. But now he did not let it rise. He looked at Madame Audubon. He kissed Rosa. Then, humming a tune, he left the room.

Chapter *4*

Off to Study

When Fougère went to bed that night, he did not go to sleep right away. He lay for a long time thinking.

He knew that his father wanted him to be a sailor or an engineer. He knew that he should not spend so much of his time watching birds. Now that he was fourteen, he ought to be studying arithmetic and geography. These were two things that every sailor and engineer should know. He ought to be studying music, which every French gentleman should know.

Fougère's father wakened him before the sun rose the next morning. Before Fougère knew what was happening, he and his father were sitting in a carriage. His trunk had been loaded in. His violin, in its case, was under his feet.

The driver took his place in the seat ahead. Soon the carriage was rattling through the city streets.

Fougère listened to the *clop, clop* of the horses' shoes. He wished his father would tell him where they were going and why.

When daylight came, Captain Audubon took a book from one of his pockets and began to read.

Fougère was left to his own thoughts. He remembered some of the things that his father had told him.

"Knowledge and hard work and honesty are more important than money," his father had often said. "Money can be lost in a short time. But knowledge cannot be taken away."

Fougère and his father traveled for several days. Finally they arrived in Rochefort, a seaport city. In front of a big house, the carriage stopped. The house was where Captain Audubon lived when he was in Rochefort on business for the French navy.

Inside the house, Captain Audubon sat down beside Fougère. He took Fougère's hand.

"My beloved boy," he said, "I have brought you here that I may be able to pay constant attention to your studies. You shall have ample time for pleasures.

But the remainder *must* be employed with industry and care.

"This day is entirely your own. I must attend to my duties. If you wish to see the docks, the fine ships-of-war, and walk around the wall, you may accompany me."

For several days, Captain Audubon tried to pay "constant attention" to his son's studies.

Then one day the Captain was ordered to go to England on navy business. Before he left, he put Fougère in the care of his secretary.

Fougère did not like the secretary. He did not like the arithmetic lessons that the secretary gave him. He did not like the room in which he studied. He felt like a prisoner of war.

One day, he slipped away from the secretary and jumped from a window into the garden below.

As his feet touched the grass, he felt free. As he walked among the trees, he felt happy again. But he did not feel free or happy for long.

The secretary had seen him jump from the window. He ordered Fougère to be put in the sailors' prison ship in the harbor. There Fougère stayed until his father came back to Rochefort.

Captain Audubon let Fougère out of prison. He scolded his son and sent him back to his studies.

After a year in Rochefort, Fougère returned to the peaceful village near Nantes. Again he roamed in the fields there. Again he drew pictures of birds.

Some of these pictures he thought good enough to keep.

When Fougère was about seventeen, his father sent him to Paris to study drawing. His teacher was Jacques Louis David, a famous French artist.

David wanted his pupils to draw pictures of old statues. Fougère wanted to draw pictures of living birds.

He was almost as unhappy in Paris as he had been in Rochefort. He stayed in Paris for only a few months. But from David he learned some things about drawing that helped him. Years later he wrote, *"David had guided my hand in tracing objects of large size."*

Chapter *5*

Off to Mill Grove

At seventeen, Fougère was no longer a boy. Now he usually signed his name Jean Jacques Audubon. He did not like the name Fougère, which means fern. Sometimes he was known as *La Forêt,* the forest. Sometimes he was known as young Audubon.

He was old enough to be fighting the British, Captain Audubon thought. The French were at war with the British, and the French navy needed men.

Young Audubon did not want to fight the British or anyone else. But he did what his father wanted him to do. He joined the French navy as a midshipman.

He made one cruise on a man-of-war. But he liked the navy even less than he liked arithmetic. As soon as peace came, he left the navy.

What should the Captain do with his son now? He thought of Mill Grove, his farm near Philadelphia. He had bought it when he was in the United States after the American Revolution.

His son should go to the United States to live on the farm. Maybe he could learn to manage it.

In the fall of 1803, Jean Jacques Audubon boarded a sailing ship bound for New York. He was now eighteen.

He hated to leave his stern but just father. He hated to leave his *chère maman,* kind, plump Madame Audubon. But he wanted to see the United States. He wanted to see Mill Grove.

Soon after he landed in New York, he became ill with yellow fever. Luckily, the captain of the sailing ship heard that the young Frenchman was sick. He took him to a boardinghouse a few miles from Philadelphia.

The boardinghouse was kept by two kind Quaker ladies. They took care of young Audubon until he was well. They taught him to speak English.

Like other Quakers of their time, they said "thee" and "thou" instead of "you."

For the rest of his life, Audubon often said "thee" and "thou" instead of "you."

At about this time, he learned to sign his name John James Audubon. He used the English words for Jean Jacques.

One day Miers Fisher, a Quaker from Philadelphia, came to see young Audubon. Mr. Fisher was an old friend of Captain Audubon. He had heard that his friend's son had been sick. He took young Audubon to his home.

Mr. Fisher was a "good and learned man." He wanted to be kind to his guest. But he was very strict. He did not like music or dancing, hunting or fishing. Audubon liked all of these things. He was unhappy without them.

"You have cared for me long enough," Audubon said to Mr. Fisher one day. "I am grateful. Now I must go to Mill Grove. It is my father's wish."

Early one morning, Mr. Fisher had his carriage brought to the door. Then he and young Audubon started off to Mill Grove. They arrived just as the sun was setting. In the fading light, Audubon could see orchards, fields with neat fences around them and a mill beside a stream.

In the big house on the hill, he met William Thomas and his wife. They were taking care of Mill Grove for Captain Audubon. Like Mr. Fisher, the Thomases were Quakers. They warmly welcomed Audubon to his father's house.

John James Audubon was about to begin one of the happiest years of his adventurous life.

"Mill Grove was ever to me a blessed spot," he wrote long afterwards.

Chapter 6

The Bakewells

It was early spring in the year 1804 when Audubon arrived at Mill Grove. Almost at once he was out in the fields and woods and along the stream. Buds were swelling on the trees, but the air was chilly. Only a few birds had come back from the south.

In the months that followed, Audubon lived a busy life. He painted pictures of birds. He fished and hunted. Each day he found something to bring home. But he did little to manage the farm.

Soon his room looked like a museum. Many birds' eggs, blown out and strung on a string, hung on the walls. Stuffed squirrels, raccoons and opossums stood on the mantelpiece. Jars of dead fish, frogs and snakes filled several shelves.

Audubon bought some beautiful horses. He rode one of them when he visited the home of a neighbor. He went to many parties and dances.

One of Audubon's near neighbors was William Bakewell, an Englishman. Mr. Bakewell and his family lived in a beautiful big house on a farm called Fatland Ford.

"Mr. Bakewell, thy neighbor, called on thee," Mrs. Thomas said one afternoon when Audubon came home from hunting. "Should thee not call on him?"

Audubon did not think he should call on Mr. Bakewell. A young Frenchman whose father had fought the British did not care to know an Englishman.

One day in late autumn, Audubon took his gun and called his dog, Zephyr. Then he set out through the snow to go hunting. Near a grove of fir trees, he met a stranger with hunting dogs and a gun. The two men talked about hunting.

The stranger, Audubon learned, was Mr. Bakewell. Audubon soon decided that Mr. Bakewell was an Englishman that a young Frenchman could like.

A few days later, Audubon rode over to Fatland Ford. Mr. Bakewell was not at home, but his daughter Lucy was there. She was sitting quietly by the fire in the parlor, sewing.

Lucy rose from her chair when Audubon came into the room.

"Will you sit down?" she asked. "My father is away, but he should be home soon. He will be happy to see you."

Lucy sat down again by the fire. Audubon sat near her. Lucy talked and sewed.

Audubon talked and looked at Lucy. He liked the pink in her cheeks. He liked her bright eyes and her gay talk.

When Mr. Bakewell came home, he seemed glad to see Audubon. He invited the young Frenchman to lunch.

As soon as lunch was over, Mr. Bakewell ordered his guns and dogs to be made ready. Then off he went with Audubon for another hunt. Audubon wondered as he left if Lucy liked him.

business partner, Ferdinand Rozier, who would help him start a store. He had 200 bird paintings he had made for Lucy.

In the summer of 1807, Audubon and Rozier traveled west to open a store in Louisville, Kentucky. The next spring, Audubon made the long journey back to Mill Grove.

He and Lucy had been engaged for more than three long years. Audubon was now 23 years old. Lucy was 20. Audubon was not yet making enough money to support a wife. But the store in Louisville had been started. The future looked bright.

Chapter 7

Storekeeper Audubon

Audubon and Lucy were married in the big house at Fatland Ford on April 12, 1808. The next day, they set out in a stagecoach for the village of Louisville.

At Pittsburgh, Audubon and Lucy left the stagecoach. There they found many people waiting for boats to take them down the Ohio River. All the boats were going west.

With other people, Audubon and Lucy boarded an ark, a big raft with a cabin built on it.

For twelve days, the ark floated down the Ohio River. As the river wound between mighty forests, Audubon and Lucy watched the birds along the bank.

At last they reached Louisville, on the south bank of the river. Audubon found his partner, Ferdinand Rozier, busy in the store. The store was doing well.

Lucy liked Louisville because people there were friendly. Audubon liked it because it had a river in front of it and forests close behind. In the river he could catch fish. In the forests he could find birds that he had not seen before.

Rozier was a good storekeeper. He spent most of his time in the store. Audubon spent most of his time hunting in the forests or drawing pictures of birds.

Sometimes Audubon spent several days in the forests without coming home.

Audubon studied the birds closely. He watched them in flight and at rest. He noticed the kinds of plants they perched on and the kinds of food they ate. He saw how they raised their families.

When Audubon drew a picture of a bird, he needed to look at it very closely. So he had to shoot it. Then he fixed it in place with wires. He tried to make it look alive.

One day when Audubon was in the store, a sad-looking stranger walked in. He was a Scotchman named Alexander Wilson. He carried two packages.

Audubon and Rozier watched as Mr. Wilson opened the packages. They gazed in surprise at what they saw.

In the packages were bird pictures that Mr. Wilson had drawn.

Mr. Wilson told Audubon he planned to put the pictures into a book as soon as he could get enough orders for it.

Audubon liked the pictures. He started to order a copy of the book, but Rozier stopped him.

"My dear Audubon," Rozier said in French, *"what induces you to subscribe to this work? Your drawings are certainly far better."*

Maybe Rozier was right, Audubon said to himself. He did not order the book. Instead, he brought out his own pictures for Mr. Wilson to see. The visitor was surprised that a wilderness storekeeper could draw so well. He was not pleased. Perhaps he was jealous.

50

For a few days, Audubon and Mr. Wilson hunted birds together. They did not like each other. Audubon was a gay Frenchman. Wilson was a sad Scot.

Later, Audubon often thought about Wilson's idea of putting bird pictures into a book.

The year after the Audubons settled in Louisville, their son Victor was born.

Soon, hard times came to the village. People had little money to spend at the store. So, when Victor was just a year old, the Audubons left Louisville. They moved downriver to a place that was later called Henderson.

There, Audubon and Rozier started another store. Again, Audubon hunted and drew pictures of birds while Rozier ran the store.

Finally, Rozier decided to sell his share of the store to Audubon. He left Henderson and moved farther west.

With Rozier gone, Audubon had little time for hunting and drawing.

The next year, the Audubons' second son, John Woodhouse, was born.

When Victor was eight years old and John was five, Audubon and several friends built a huge mill. The mill was for grinding wheat and corn and for sawing trees into lumber. It was so big that people came for miles to see it. But it was not a success.

Audubon lost so much money on the mill that he was put in prison for debt. When he came out of prison, he had only his clothes, his gun, his family and his pictures of birds.

Chapter *8*

Hard Times

After Audubon came out of prison, he and Lucy talked over what he should do. They decided he should stop being part storekeeper and part artist. He should paint even more bird pictures. In a few years he would have enough pictures for a book.

Lucy knew that Audubon would have to look for new birds to paint. He would have to be away from home for months at a time. For a while, Lucy would have to earn money to help support the family.

Audubon's friends said unkind things about him. Some said, "He's not looking after his family." Others said, "He's just wasting his time wandering in the woods and painting pictures."

Lucy did not mind what people said. She believed that some day Audubon would be known to the world as a great bird artist. Victor and John agreed.

"My best friends solemnly regarded me as a madman," Audubon wrote a few years later. *"My wife and family alone gave me encouragement."*

On an October day in 1820, Audubon left his family in Kentucky and set out on a flatboat for New Orleans. Down the Ohio River and then down the Mississippi River he traveled with two friends and his dog, Dash.

Audubon saw many birds he had not seen before. He stopped the flatboat often so that he could paint pictures of them. When he reached New Orleans, he had no money, but he had many paintings of birds.

The next three years were hard ones for the Audubons. Sometimes they were together. More often they were apart. They never had much money.

Lucy helped to support the family by teaching school. She taught first in a city in southern Ohio. Later, she and the boys moved to Louisiana. There she taught children who lived on cotton and sugar plantations.

Audubon worked hard. Often he worked sixteen hours a day. Often he slept only four hours at night.

He earned money by giving drawing lessons and by painting many pictures of people.

One day Audubon found that 200 of his bird paintings being shipped in a box had been badly damaged. Even this sad accident did not discourage him.

In the autumn of 1823, Audubon decided to go to Philadelphia. There he hoped to find a printer who would make his bird paintings into a book.

He left Lucy and John in Louisiana, at a place called Bayou Sara. He and fourteen-year-old Victor set out for the north. They traveled part way by steamboat, part way on foot and part way by horse and wagon. Audubon left Victor with relatives in Kentucky. He went alone to Philadelphia.

Summer Red Bird Male old Young.

TANAGRA ÆSTIVA.

Plant Vulgo Wild Muscadine.

Chapter 9

In Search of a Printer

In Philadelphia, Audubon met Charles Bonaparte, a nephew of Napoleon, the Emperor of France. Young Bonaparte was writing a book on birds. He introduced Audubon to many scientists and artists.

Soon Audubon's bird paintings were hanging in the famous Academy of Natural Sciences. Many people came to see them. Most of the people thought that Audubon's paintings were the most beautiful bird pictures they had ever seen. His pictures had both birds and plants in them. The birds were life-size.

A few of the scientists and artists were jealous of Audubon.

"Why do you put plants in the pictures with your birds?" one of the scientists asked Audubon. "No real scientist would do that."

"I draw birds as I see them in the forests," Audubon said. "I do not draw them as you see them in a museum."

"Audubon is right," young Bonaparte said. "His birds look alive. They are as we see them in nature."

Audubon could find no printer in Philadelphia good enough to make his pictures into a book.

"You must go to Europe," Bonaparte told him. "There you will find better printers."

Audubon felt discouraged.

He had no money for a trip to Europe. He went to New York City and then up the Hudson River. In the northern forests he hoped to find birds he had never seen before.

All alone in the pathless forests, he thought of young Bonaparte's advice. Yes, he decided, he would take his pictures to Europe. He would have them made into a book called *The Birds of America*. But first he would have to paint still more pictures for the book. Also, he would have to earn money for the trip.

After visiting Niagara Falls, Audubon started toward Louisiana. He arrived at Bayou Sara by steamboat late in the month of November.

Eagerly he told Lucy his plans.

"I will help you," Lucy said. In the fourteen months Audubon had been away, she had saved some money. She had been teaching.

Audubon now went to work to earn still more money. For more than a year he taught French, music, dancing and drawing. His pupils were boys and girls who lived near Lucy's home at Bayou Sara.

On April 26, 1826, Audubon wrote in his diary: *"I left My Beloved Wife Lucy and My Son John Woodhouse on Tuesday afternoon the 26th April, bound to England."*

Three weeks and a day later, he and 400 bird pictures were aboard the good ship *Delos*. Seven years had passed since Audubon had gone to prison for debt.

Chapter *10*

A Printer Found

A week after landing in England, Audubon was invited to exhibit his pictures at the Royal Institution in Liverpool. Many people came to the exhibit—413 in one day. Some came to see the pictures. Some came to see John James Audubon.

This American woodsman made them curious. He wore rough clothes, and he let his wavy black hair flow over his shoulders. He rose early, worked late, ate simple food and took no strong drink.

From Liverpool, Audubon traveled to Edinburgh, Scotland. He was welcomed warmly. When his pictures were shown there, he became the talk of the city.

A Frenchman who saw the pictures wrote: *"A magic power transported us into the forests which for so many years this man of genius has trod."*

Audubon was invited to dinners, teas and even breakfasts. He was made a member of famous scientific and art societies.

"My situation in Edinburgh borders on the miraculous," he wrote to Lucy. *"I go out to dine at six, seven, or even eight o'clock in the evening, and it is often one or two when the party breaks up. Then painting all day makes my head feel like an immense hornet's-nest."*

One of the first people Audubon met in Edinburgh was W. Home Lizars, a printer.

"I never saw anything like this before," Mr. Lizars said when he saw Audubon's pictures. He agreed to make the pictures into a book called *The Birds of America.*

"Mr. Audubon," he said, "the people here don't know who you are at all, but depend upon it, they *shall* know."

Making a colored picture book in 1826 took a long time.

The first of Audubon's pictures that Mr. Lizars printed was the wild turkey-cock. The turkey on the paper was as large as the real turkeys in America.

Audubon decided he could not have all of his pictures printed at one time.

Photo from National Audubon Society

They cost too much. He would have five made each year. He would take orders for them.

From Edinburgh, Audubon went to London. He was welcomed there also. Many people had parties for him. They admired his pictures. Some of them ordered copies of his book. Even the Queen ordered a copy.

Soon Audubon had bad news. Mr. Lizars' workmen had left him.

Audubon began looking for someone in London who would print his pictures. He felt discouraged.

"Oh, how sick I am of London!" he wrote to Lucy.

At last, Audubon met Mr. Robert Havell, Jr. Young Mr. Havell was in the printing business with his father.

Robert Havell & Son were even better printers than Mr. Lizars. They said they would print *The Birds of America*.

But Audubon's troubles were not over. The printing of his pictures went slowly. He had very little money. He worked harder than ever. He got up at four o'clock in the morning to paint.

"I painted all day, and sold my work during the dusky hours of the evening as I walked through the Strand and other streets," he wrote.

Most of the pictures he painted were of birds. Some were of foxes, otters, dogs and lambs. He painted any picture he thought people would buy.

Some of the people who had promised to buy copies of his *Birds of America* broke their promises. Then Audubon had to leave London to find other people who would order his book.

Three days after Audubon's second Christmas in England, the fifth part of *The Birds of America* came from the printer. *"The work pleased me quite,"* Audubon wrote to Lucy. Twenty-five of the bird pictures had now been printed.

From England, Audubon wrote long letters to Lucy. Many letters began, *"My Dearest Friend and Wife."* One letter ended, *"Good night my Dearest Love and friend."* Another ended, *"Now Good Night my dearest Lucy. I must put my sore feet in warm water and go to bed. God bless you all."*

In one letter, Audubon told Lucy, *"Do remember my beloved wife to teach (no matter how unwilling he may be)*

70

our Johny the piano and see that his Drawing goes on regularly and well."

Three years after Audubon landed in England, he came back to America.

He spent a year visiting his family and painting more pictures of birds. Then he went back to London. This time, Lucy went with him.

In London, Audubon found that he had been made a Fellow of the Royal Society. After that, he sometimes wrote his name, *"John James Audubon, F.R.S."* He was very proud of these letters at the end of his name. They meant that he was one of the great scientists of the world.

Chapter *11*

Success at Last

Audubon and Lucy were very happy. They were in England together. They were no longer poor. Audubon was now famous. But he did not stop working. He started another book.

In the new book, Audubon wrote about the birds he had painted for *The Birds of America*. He told where and how the birds lived. Lucy and a young Scotchman helped him.

When Audubon finished his first book on the lives of the birds, he and Lucy hurried back to the United States.

Audubon needed more pictures for *The Birds of America* that young Mr. Havell was printing. He wanted to visit places in the south and north and west, and paint birds he had not seen before.

With two helpers, Audubon set out for Florida. On the way, he met John Bachman, a minister who was living in Charleston, South Carolina. Bachman was a scientist as well as a minister. He and Audubon became great friends.

In Florida, Audubon and his helpers waded for days through swamps and salt marshes. The weather was stormy. Once they were almost drowned.

"Where all that is not mud, mud, mud, is sand, sand, sand," Audubon wrote in a letter. He saw only a few new birds.

He hoped to find new birds in other places. With Lucy, Victor and John, he traveled north along the coast of Maine.

Victor was then 23 years old. John was almost 20. Audubon decided they were old enough to help him.

Both Victor and John could draw, paint and write very well. From that time on, Victor had charge of the business of printing and selling the books. John went with his father on long trips and helped him collect birds to paint. Both sons helped Audubon paint pictures and write books.

When Audubon went to Labrador, on the rocky eastern coast of Canada, he took John with him. He tried to cure John of his habit of sleeping late by calling him every morning at four.

In Labrador the weather was rainy, and Audubon often worked in damp clothes. On some days he worked for seventeen hours. He complained because his shoulders and fingers grew tired.

At the end of two months in the wild and grand country of Labrador, Audubon had 23 large drawings to add to *The Birds of America*.

In 1838, twelve years after Audubon first sailed for England, *The Birds of America* was finished.

On its 435 pages, it had pictures of 1,065 birds. Every bird was pictured as Audubon had seen it outdoors. Every bird was its real size.

Audubon felt very happy. He and Lucy celebrated by taking a vacation trip in the highlands of Scotland.

The next year, Audubon's fifth book on the lives of birds was printed. Then Audubon and Reverend Bachman began working on books about the four-footed animals of North America.

Audubon did not like to live in a city. He bought a small farm on the east bank of the Hudson River. It was north of the New York City of his time. He called it "Minnie's Land," in honor of Lucy. "Minnie" is a Scotch word for "mother."

There Audubon built a large house. It was near the present 155th Street of New York City. There he spent most of the rest of his life. He took trips to England and Scotland and to far places in the United States. But he always returned joyfully to Minnie's Land.

Audubon had long wanted to see the Far West. When he was 58 years old, he and four friends traveled hundreds of miles up the Missouri River. They went as far as the Yellowstone River.

Once Audubon wrote in his notebook: *"Buffaloes all over the prairies. The roaring can be heard for miles."*

He was nearly gored by a wild buffalo that had been wounded.

Audubon saw some animals he had never seen before. He painted pictures of many of them. Later some of the pictures were printed in the books on four-footed animals.

The trip to the Far West was the last great journey for the great traveler.

Audubon spent the rest of his life quietly with Lucy at Minnie's Land.

His sons, Victor and John, lived with their families in big houses nearby.

Several years after Audubon died, a stone monument in memory of him was put up in a churchyard. It was near Minnie's Land. But people do not need a stone monument to remind them of Audubon. His true and most lasting monument is *The Birds of America,* which all the world loves and admires.

Audubon was a man who knew what he wanted to do. He believed he could do it. With Lucy's help, he did it.